Get Dressed!

Gwenyth Swain

First Avenue Editions/Minneapolis

To find out more about the pictures in this book, turn to page 22.
To find out more about sharing this book with children, turn to page 24.

The photographs in this book are reproduced through the courtesy of: © CORBIS Royalty Free, front cover and p. 4; © Glacial Lakes and Prairies of Northeastern South Dakota, back cover and p. 7; © Tiziana and Gianni Baldizzone/CORBIS, p. 1; © Todd Gipstein/CORBIS, P. 3; © Dean Conger/CORBIS, pp. 5, 15; © CORBIS Royalty Free, p. 6; © Julie Habel/CORBIS, p. 8; © David and Peter Tumley/CORBIS, p. 9; © Jodi Jacobson/Peter Arnold, p. 10; © Morton Beebe, S.F./CORBIS, p. 11; © Penny Tweedie/CORBIS, p. 12; © Françoise Gervais/CORBIS, p. 13; © Pablo Corral V/CORBIS, p. 14; © Reflections Photolibrary/CORBIS, pp. 16, 18; © Laura Dwight/CORBIS, p. 17; © Phil Schermeister/CORBIS, p. 19; © Philip Gould/CORBIS, p. 20; © Liba Taylor/CORBIS, p. 21.

First Avenue Editions
An imprint of Lerner Publishing Group, Inc.
241 First Avenue North
Minneapolis, MN 55401 U.S.A.

Website address: www.lernerbooks.com

Library of Congress Cataloging-in-Publication Data

Swain, Gwenyth, 1961-
    Get Dressed! / by Gwenyth Swain.
      p.   cm. — (Small world)
    Includes index.
    ISBN-13: 978–1–57505–159–8 (pbk. : alk. paper)
    ISBN-10: 1–57505–159–1 (pbk. : alk. paper)
    1. Children—Life skills guides—Juvenile literature. I. Title.
  II. Small world (Minneapolis, Minn.)
  HQ781.S93 2002
  305.23—dc21   2001003598

Manufactured in the United States of America
6 –VI – 2/1/11

What do you like to wear?

Do your clothes hang loose?

Do they hug you tight?

Does a special outfit make
you look just right?

Pick clothes to fit you
and the things you do.

Pull on a parka to play in snow.

Cover yourself, but
let your smile show.

Choose clothes with care
when you want to stay cool.

Slip into a suit and splash at the pool.

Beads and paint say it's your big day.

The slant of a hat says it's time to play.

Grab clean, dry clothes
fresh from the line.

Pull them on or press them.
You'll look fine.

Tug on your zipper. Cover your toes.

Loop and pull to make a neat bow.

Button that button.

Tie that tie.

Get ready. Get dressed!

Add a smile. Look your best.

More about the Pictures

Front cover and page 4: Loose clothing keeps friends cool in the hot climate of Tanzania, a country in East Africa.

Back cover and page 7: A young powwow dancer performs in South Dakota.

Page 1: A Rabari girl is dressed for her naming ceremony in the state of Gujarat in western India.

Page 3: A girl in Beijing, China, wears her school uniform—and a smile.

Page 5: A toddler is bundled up tight for a winter day in Irkutsk, Russia.

Page 6: Two girls on the Indonesian island of Bali wear ceremonial dresses and headdresses.

Page 8: Children in New Vienna, Iowa, dress warmly to play in the snow.

Page 9: A young girl in Tehran, Iran, wears *hijab*, or Islamic dress that covers all but her face and hands. The word *hijab* comes from the Arabic word for modesty.

Page 10: A girl in New Jersey picks an outfit for a hot summer day.

Page 11: A young girl floats on a raft in a swimming pool in Puerto Vallarta, Mexico.

Page 12: These two Aboriginal boys in Arnhem Land, a region in northern Australia, are dressed for a ceremony. The Aborigines were the earliest known people to live in Australia.

Page 13: Girls play dress-up in Naskeag, Maine.

Page 14: Clothes dry on the line outside a traditional house along the Tomebamba River in Cuenca, Ecuador.

Page 15: A West Indian girl carries a bundle of laundry on her head in Grenadines, Windward Islands.

Page 16: This young girl is just learning to pull socks snug over her toes.

Page 17: This American boy knows how to tie his shoelaces. Do you know how?

Page 18: An English girl buttons her school blazer.

Page 19: Boys on North Caicos Island in the Bahamas help each other look their best for their graduation ceremony.

Page 20: In Saint George, Bermuda, two eight-year-olds start the day right in neat, clean clothes.

Page 21: In the Gambia, a country in West Africa, a girl keeps her head covered and her eyes and smile bright.

A Note to Adults on Sharing This Book

Help your child become a lifelong reader. Read this book together, taking turns as you both read out loud. Look over the photographs and choose your favorites. Sound out new words and come back to them later for review. Then try these "extensions"—activities that extend the experience of reading and build discussion and problem-solving skills.

Talk about Getting Dressed
All around the world, people wear clothes that suit the weather and suit the things they do. Ask your child to describe the clothing people wear in this book. How do the outfits differ from what your child wears? How are they the same? Ask your child why children in different parts of the world wear different clothes. What kinds of outfits shown in the book would your child like to wear for a change?

Make a Paper "Closet"
With your child, gather pictures of people dressed in different ways. Copy photographs of yourself as a child wearing your favorite outfits. Ask your child to cut out pictures of unusual-looking clothes from magazines. Then put all the pictures together in a scrapbook. Think of this book as a paper "closet." Ask your child what clothes he or she would take out of the closet and wear in the summer or winter, on Halloween or to school, or for a party or special event.